United States Presidents

Thomas Jefferson

Anne Welsbacher

ABDO Publishing Company

JB
Jefferson
Welsbacher

visit us at
www.abdopub.com

Published by Abdo Publishing Company 4940 Viking Drive, Edina, Minnesota 55435.
Copyright © 1999 by Abdo Consulting Group, Inc. International copyrights reserved in
all countries. No part of this book may be reproduced in any form without written
permission from the publisher.

Printed in the United States.

Cover and Interior Photo credits: AP/Wide World, Archive, Corbis-Bettmann

Contributing editors: Robert Italia, Tamara L. Britton, K. M. Brielmaier
Book design/maps: Patrick Laurel

Library of Congress Cataloging-in-Publication Data

Welsbacher, Anne, 1955-
    Thomas Jefferson / Anne Welsbacher.
       p. cm. -- (United States presidents)
    Includes index.
    Summary: Presents the life story of the third president of the United States, who
authored the Declaration of Independence and is known for his ability as an
inventor and architect.
    ISBN 1-56239-809-1
    1. Jefferson, Thomas, 1743-1826--Juvenile literature. 2. Presidents--United
States--Biography--Juvenile literature. [1. Jefferson, Thomas, 1743-1826. 2.
Presidents.] I. Title. II. Series: United States presidents (Edina, Minn.)
E322.79.W45 1999
973.4'6'092--dc21
    [B]   98-11016
                                                CIP
                                                AC

Contents

President of the People

*T*homas Jefferson was the third president of the United States. He helped create America. And he fought for human rights.

Thomas Jefferson was born in Virginia. He liked the outdoors. He also liked music and dancing. Thomas studied many books and subjects. He went to college and studied law. In 1772, he married Martha Wayles Skelton.

In the 1770s, the colonies fought Great Britain for their freedom. In 1776, Jefferson wrote the **Declaration of Independence**. This **document** said that America was a new country. Jefferson also helped pass many laws in Virginia that gave people new rights.

In 1782, Martha Jefferson died. Jefferson was very sad for a long time. He raised his daughters by himself, and never remarried.

Jefferson worked in France for many years. Later, he became **secretary of state**. He also helped form the new **Democratic-Republican** party.

In 1801, Jefferson was elected president. He bought a huge amount of land that made the U.S. twice as big. Then he sent explorers west to learn about this land.

Jefferson served two terms as president. Then he returned home. He read books, started a new college, and built many inventions. He died on July 4, 1826. It was the 50th birthday of the United States.

Thomas Jefferson worked hard for freedom of religion and freedom of speech. These are important rights in America. He also worked for equal rights for all Americans, not just rich people. For this reason, he sometimes is called "Man of the People."

Thomas Jefferson

Thomas Jefferson (1743-1826)
Third President

BORN:	April 13, 1743
PLACE OF BIRTH:	Shadwell, Albemarle County, Virginia
ANCESTRY:	Welsh
FATHER:	Peter Jefferson (1708-1757)
MOTHER:	Jane Randolph Jefferson (1720-1776)
WIFE:	Martha Wayles Skelton (Patty) (1748-1782)
CHILDREN:	Six: 1 boy, 5 girls
EDUCATION:	Private tutoring; country school in Albemarle; College of William and Mary
RELIGION:	No formal membership
OCCUPATION:	Lawyer, inventor, author
MILITARY SERVICE:	Colonel of County Militia, Virginia
POLITICAL PARTY:	Democratic-Republican

OFFICES HELD:	Served in Virginia legislature; county lieutenant; county surveyor; delegate to First and Second Continental Congress; member of Virginia's delegation to Congress; governor of Virginia; commissioner to France; minister to France; secretary of state; vice president
AGE AT INAUGURATION:	57
YEARS SERVED:	1801-1805, 1805-1809
VICE PRESIDENT:	Aaron Burr (1801-1805) and George Clinton (1805-1809)
DIED:	July 4, 1826, Charlottesville, Virginia, age 83
CAUSE OF DEATH:	Natural causes

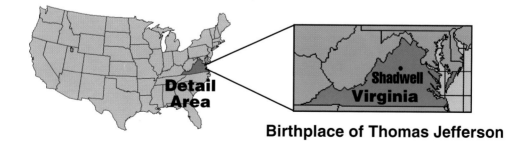

Birthplace of Thomas Jefferson

Early Years

*T*homas Jefferson was born in Shadwell, Virginia, on April 13, 1743. Virginia was a British colony.

Thomas's father, Peter, had many jobs. He earned money making maps of the Virginia wilderness. Thomas's mother, Jane, was from a wealthy southern family.

Thomas had six sisters and a brother. When Thomas was two years old, the family moved to a nearby **plantation**.

When he was five, Thomas learned lessons from a **tutor**. When Thomas was nine, his family returned to Shadwell. Thomas went to a school at Dover Church.

In school, Thomas learned many languages. He learned the names of trees and plants. And he learned to play the violin. Thomas liked dancing, reading, and canoeing.

When Thomas was 14, his father died. Peter left Thomas much of his wealth. But Thomas was sad. He had been close to his father. Now he felt lost and alone with no one to guide him through life.

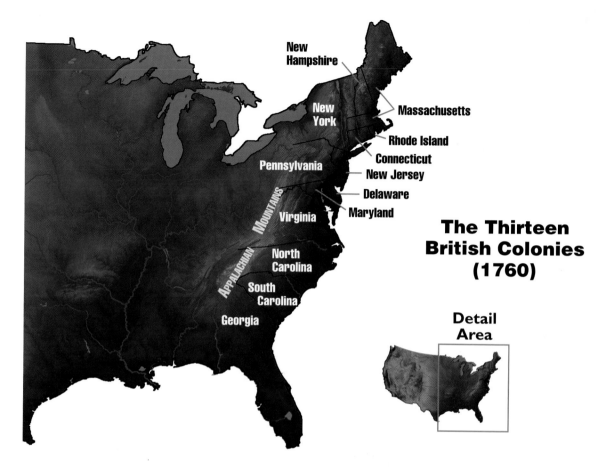

The Thirteen
British Colonies
(1760)

Detail
Area

*The Appalachian Mountains formed the
western limits of the British colonies.*

Thomas went to the Reverend James Maury's classical
school. He studied long hours and learned to write well. He
practiced the violin. And he learned Greek and Latin. Maury
gave Thomas the guidance he needed.

Law and Politics

*I*n March 1760, Jefferson went to the College of William and Mary in Williamsburg, Virginia. He read many books. He made new friends. They played music and studied hard. They discussed religion, science, and math.

Jefferson left college after two years. He studied law at a Williamsburg law office. He also traveled to Shadwell to help run the **plantation**.

In 1765, Great Britain passed a new law called the Stamp Act. Now, colonists had to pay a new tax on goods from other countries. Many colonists were angry.

Jefferson heard a speech by his friend, Patrick Henry. Henry was a **legislator**. He believed that the colonies should fight Great Britain. Jefferson became interested in politics. He was excited about freedom for America.

In 1767, Jefferson became a lawyer. But his interest in politics remained strong. In 1769, Jefferson was elected to the Virginia **legislature**. He wrote many laws to help Virginians.

Many of the laws he wrote for Virginia were used later in the U.S. Constitution. Today, Americans enjoy freedom of religion, free public education, and public libraries thanks to Thomas Jefferson.

Thomas Jefferson studied to be a lawyer.

Monticello and Congress

*I*n 1769, Jefferson started to build a new house near Shadwell. It was on a small Virginia mountain called *Monticello*, which is the Italian word for "little mountain." Jefferson owned the land atop Monticello. His father left Jefferson this land when he died.

The next year, Jefferson met Martha Wayles Skelton. Thomas and Martha loved music. They played songs and sang together. They were married on January 1, 1772.

Thomas and Martha lived at Monticello. They had many slaves. Both **inherited** slaves from their fathers. Jefferson did not support slavery. He called it a crime. He felt all people should be free.

Monticello, home of Thomas Jefferson

Jefferson tried to pass laws in Virginia that would free all slaves. But the laws did not pass. Jefferson was afraid to free his slaves. He feared they would be mistreated. So, he kept them. But he vowed to treat his slaves well. He improved their food, clothing, and housing.

In 1773, angry colonists threw British tea into Boston Harbor to protest a tea tax. This was called the Boston Tea Party. American leaders met in Philadelphia in 1774. They discussed taxes and independence. This meeting was called the First Continental **Congress**.

Jefferson was ill and did not go to the meeting. But he sent letters that explained why the colonies should be independent.

In May 1775, Jefferson went to the Second Continental Congress. By then, fighting had begun between the colonies and Great Britain. Jefferson wrote many letters to the British. He protested their actions and defended the colonists.

The congress chose George Washington to lead the new American army. It also acted as the colonies' new government. The congress issued money, set up a postal service, and created a navy. The **American Revolution** had begun.

The Making of the Third United States President

1743
Born April 13, in Shadwell, Virginia

1748
Learns school lessons from a tutor

1752
Starts school at Dover Church

1757
Father dies

1760
Enters the College of William and Mary in Williamsburg, Virginia

1772
Marries Martha Wayles Skelton

1775
Attends Second Continental Congress

1776
Writes the Declaration of Independence

1779
Elected Governor of Virginia

1781
Escapes capture by the British army

1790
Made the secretary of state by George Washington

1796
Elected vice president of the U.S.

1801
Congress elects Jefferson president of the U.S.

1803
Louisiana Purchase

1804
Re-elected as president

PRESIDENTIAL YEARS

Thomas Jefferson

"We hold these truths to be self-evident: that all men are created equal, that they are endowed by their Creator with certain inalienable rights, among these are life, liberty, and the pursuit of happiness. . . . "

1762
Studies law

1767
Admitted to the Virginia Bar

1769
Elected to the Virginia Legislature

Historic Events
during Jefferson's Presidency

★ Ohio admitted to the Union

★ Gas lighting introduced in Europe

★ Slave trade outlawed in England

1782
Wife Martha dies

1784
Moves to France, stays for five years

1785
Made minister to France

1808
James Madison is elected president

1815
Sells library to Congress

1819
Starts the University of Virginia

1825
The University of Virginia opens

1826
Dies July 4, fifty years after the Declaration of Independence is signed

Independence

*I*n the summer of 1776, John Adams asked Thomas Jefferson to write a **document**. **Congress** wanted to declare to the world that the colonies were free and independent states.

Jefferson wrote the document in only a few days. On July 4, 1776, Congress signed it. Americans still celebrate the signing of the **Declaration of Independence** every year on the fourth of July.

That fall, Jefferson returned to Virginia. He worked for better state laws. These laws gave Virginians the right to own land. Virginians also received the right to an education. And they could not be punished because of their religion.

In 1779, Jefferson was elected governor of Virginia. The next year, the British army invaded the state. Jefferson barely escaped capture in 1781. Many Virginians criticized Governor Jefferson for his actions during the invasion. So, Jefferson quit.

Later that year, the British army became trapped at Yorktown, Virginia. Their leader, General Charles Cornwallis, surrendered to General Washington. The **American Revolution** was over.

In September 1782, Martha died. Jefferson was very sad. He continued to work in politics. But he never married again.

In 1784, Jefferson went to France as a U.S. **diplomat**. His daughter, Martha, went with him. His daughter Polly arrived later.

The next year, Jefferson became the minister to France. He met with European leaders to write treaties. He helped spread American business through Europe. He studied European **culture**. And he saw the start of the **French Revolution**. Jefferson and his daughters returned to America in 1789.

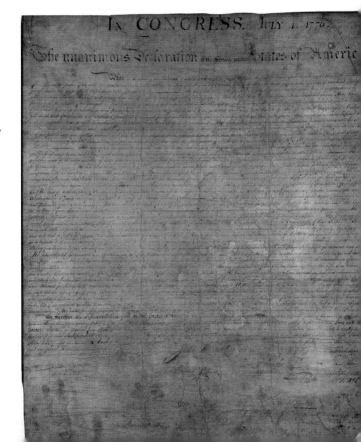

The Declaration of Independence

Two New Parties

*I*n 1789, President George Washington asked Jefferson to join his **cabinet**. Jefferson would be the first U.S. **secretary of state**. The offer troubled Jefferson. He felt that no person had the right to "choose his post."

Washington convinced Jefferson that Americans needed him. Jefferson knew how to work with other countries. In 1790, he accepted the offer.

Jefferson often battled with the **secretary of the treasury**, Alexander Hamilton. Hamilton was a Federalist. Federalists believed that a strong national government should rule the country.

Jefferson felt that a strong national government was against the Constitution. To fight the Federalists, Jefferson and his supporters formed a political group. They called it the **Democratic-Republicans**.

President Washington often sided with Hamilton. Jefferson grew frustrated. He quit in 1794 and returned home to be a farmer.

For the next three years, Jefferson worked on Monticello. He designed new plans for his house and made it twice as big. He came up with a new way to rotate crops. And he improved the plow and the **thresher**.

In 1796, it was time to elect a new U.S. president. Jefferson ran as a **Democratic-Republican**. John Adams ran as a Federalist, and won. Jefferson finished second, and became vice president.

In 1798, **Congress** passed the Sedition Act. It became illegal for anyone to speak against the government. Jefferson called the law unconstitutional. He convinced the Virginia and Kentucky **legislatures** to vote down the law in their states.

In 1800, Jefferson ran for president again. This time, he tied Aaron Burr. By law, Congress had to break the tie. On February 17, 1801, Jefferson was elected the third president of the United States.

Alexander Hamilton

President Jefferson

*P*resident Thomas Jefferson worked hard to support the freedoms he believed in. Newspapers printed hateful stories about him. But he did not punish the people who wrote the stories. He thought people should be free to write what they believed. This is called freedom of the press.

Jefferson helped change laws the Federalists had passed when John Adams was president. He lowered taxes and cut the size of the army. And he swept many Federalists from office.

But there were problems abroad. Pirates often attacked American ships off the North African coast. As commander-in-chief, Jefferson ordered the U.S. Navy to protect the ships.

In 1803, France owned all the land between the Mississippi River and the Rocky Mountains. This land was called the Louisiana Territory. But France was in a costly war with Great Britain. France needed to sell the land to make money.

Jefferson bought the land for the United States. It was called the Louisiana Purchase.

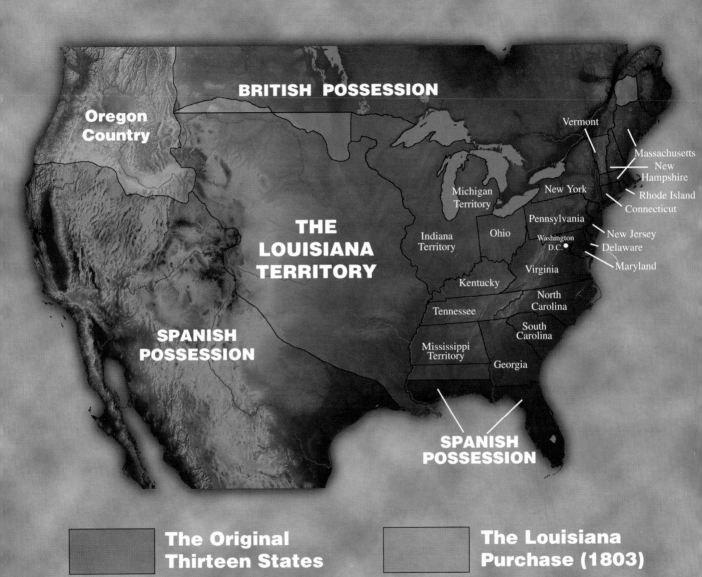

BRITISH POSSESSION

Oregon
Country

**THE
LOUISIANA
TERRITORY**

Vermont

Massachusetts
New
Hampshire

New York

Rhode Island
Connecticut

Michigan
Territory

Pennsylvania

New Jersey

Indiana
Territory

Ohio

Washington
D.C.

Delaware

Virginia

Maryland

Kentucky

North
Carolina

Tennessee

South
Carolina

**SPANISH
POSSESSION**

Mississippi
Territory

Georgia

**SPANISH
POSSESSION**

The Original
Thirteen States

The Louisiana
Purchase (1803)

U.S. States or
Territories

Land Claimed by
U.S. and Britain

The Louisiana Purchase made the United States twice as big. Now, America was larger than any country in Europe.

Jefferson sent his nephew Meriwether Lewis and William Clark to explore the new land. The Lewis and Clark Expedition discovered plants and animals never written of before. When they returned, they told Jefferson of America's new natural wonders.

In 1804, President Jefferson was re-elected. He was the first president to be **inaugurated** in Washington, D.C., which he helped design. The national government had been in Philadelphia, Pennsylvania. Jefferson also was the first to start a term in the new White House.

During his second term, Jefferson stopped the Southwest Territory from leaving the Union. He also signed a law that stopped all shipment of slaves into the country.

Meriwether Lewis

In 1808, the **Democratic-Republicans** wanted Jefferson to run for a third term. He refused. Jefferson felt being president should not be a lifelong job. He helped James Madison run for president. When Madison won, Jefferson returned to Monticello.

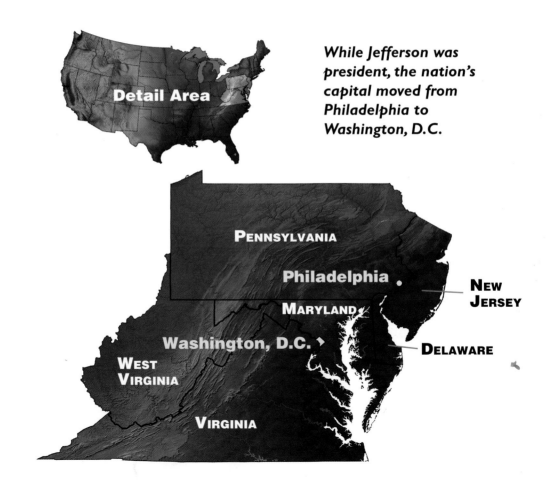

While Jefferson was president, the nation's capital moved from Philadelphia to Washington, D.C.

Detail Area

PENNSYLVANIA

Philadelphia

NEW JERSEY

MARYLAND

DELAWARE

Washington, D.C.

WEST VIRGINIA

VIRGINIA

The Seven "Hats" of the U.S. President

A president can serve only two terms. Each term lasts four years. When Jefferson was president, this law did not exist.

A president is elected or re-elected every four years.

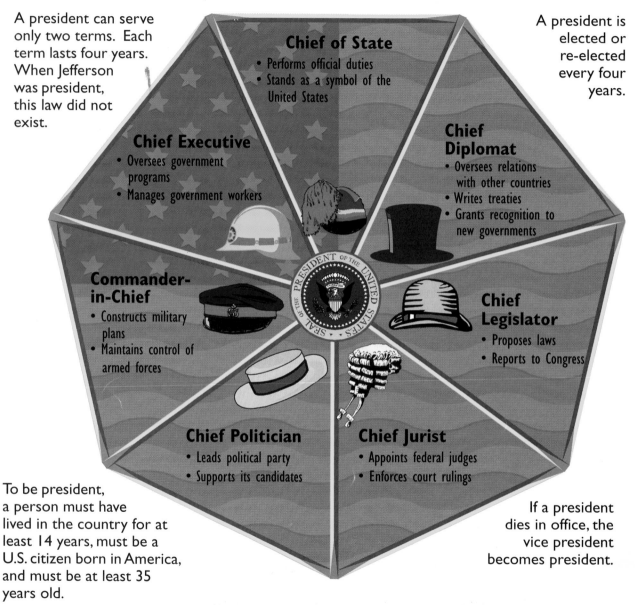

Chief of State
- Performs official duties
- Stands as a symbol of the United States

Chief Executive
- Oversees government programs
- Manages government workers

Chief Diplomat
- Oversees relations with other countries
- Writes treaties
- Grants recognition to new governments

Commander-in-Chief
- Constructs military plans
- Maintains control of armed forces

Chief Legislator
- Proposes laws
- Reports to Congress

Chief Politician
- Leads political party
- Supports its candidates

Chief Jurist
- Appoints federal judges
- Enforces court rulings

To be president, a person must have lived in the country for at least 14 years, must be a U.S. citizen born in America, and must be at least 35 years old.

If a president dies in office, the vice president becomes president.

As president, Thomas Jefferson had seven jobs.

The Three Branches of the U.S. Government

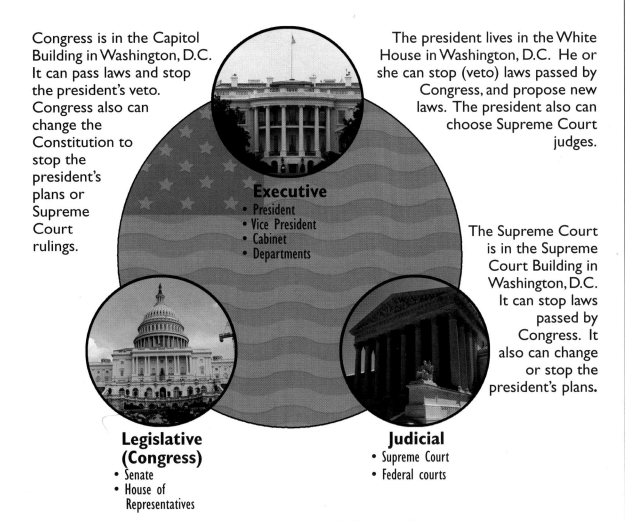

Congress is in the Capitol Building in Washington, D.C. It can pass laws and stop the president's veto. Congress also can change the Constitution to stop the president's plans or Supreme Court rulings.

The president lives in the White House in Washington, D.C. He or she can stop (veto) laws passed by Congress, and propose new laws. The president also can choose Supreme Court judges.

The Supreme Court is in the Supreme Court Building in Washington, D.C. It can stop laws passed by Congress. It also can change or stop the president's plans.

Executive
- President
- Vice President
- Cabinet
- Departments

Legislative (Congress)
- Senate
- House of Representatives

Judicial
- Supreme Court
- Federal courts

The U.S. Constitution was written in 1787. It formed three government branches. Each branch has power over the others. So, no single group or person can control the country. The Constitution calls this "separation of powers." Jefferson first wrote these ideas in the Virginia Constitution in 1783.

The University

At Monticello, Jefferson kept busy. He drew up more plans for the house and gardens. He saw guests each day. He wrote many letters, read books, and did science projects.

During the **War of 1812**, British soldiers burned the Library of **Congress**. Jefferson sold his Monticello library to Congress in 1815. Then he started buying more books.

Jefferson invented new things. He made a moving shelf to carry bottles from his wine cellar to his kitchen. He made a machine that could copy letters as he wrote them.

In 1819, Jefferson started the University of Virginia. He helped design the buildings and choose textbooks. And he raised money to pay for the school.

Before his death, Jefferson asked that three lines be carved on his gravestone. They were: Author of the Declaration of American Independence, Author of the Virginia Statute for Religious Freedom, and Father of the University of Virginia.

Thomas Jefferson started the University of Virginia.

On July 4, 1826, Thomas Jefferson died. He was 83. John Adams died the same day. It was exactly 50 years after the signing of the **Declaration of Independence**.

Fun Facts

- Jefferson was tall, thin, and strong. His school friends called him "Long Tom."

- In the 1700s, Americans celebrated each president's birthday. President Jefferson thought that was too much fuss—so he did not tell anybody when he was born.

- Jefferson created the coin system we use today. The British system that the colonists used made one pound equal 20 shillings, or 240 pence. Jefferson divided dollars into 10 dimes or 100 pennies, which was much easier to count and exchange.

- Jefferson invented many things during his lifetime. He installed a "turning machine" in his closet that held his clothes. And he had ideas for a stopwatch and a submarine. Jefferson liked inventions that made daily life easier.

- Jefferson was the first president to shake hands with White House visitors. People bowed to the first two presidents, but Jefferson did not want to be treated like a king.

The Jefferson Memorial in Washington, D.C.

Glossary

American Revolution - 1775-1783. A war between Great Britain and its colonies in America. The Americans won their independence and created the United States.

cabinet - a group of advisers chosen by the president.

Congress - the lawmaking body of the U.S. It is made up of the House of Representatives and the Senate.

culture - the customs, arts, and tools of a nation or people.

Declaration of Independence - an important paper saying that the American colonies were free and would start their own government.

Democratic-Republican - a political party in the early 1800s that believed in weak national government and strong state government.

diplomat - a person who deals with representatives of other countries.

document - a paper, usually for an important purpose.

French Revolution - 1789-1799. The people of France overthrew the king and set up a new democratic government.

inaugurate - to be sworn into office.

inherit - to get or have something after the last owner dies.

legislator - someone who makes and passes laws.

legislature - the lawmaking group of a state or country.

plantation - a large farm.

secretary of state - a member of the president's cabinet who handles problems with other countries.

secretary of the treasury - the head of the U.S. Treasury department who helps decide economic matters.

thresh - to separate kernels from wheat, rye, or other grains.

tutor - a private teacher.

War of 1812 - 1812-1814. A war between America and Great Britain over shipping and the capture of sailors.

Internet Sites

PBS American Presidents Series
http://www.americanpresidents.org
Visit the PBS Web site which features the biographies of each president. Check out the key events of each presidency, speeches, fun facts, and trivia games.

Welcome to the White House
http://www.whitehouse.gov
The official Web site of the White House. After an introduction from the current president of the United States, the site takes you through biographies of each president. Get information on White House history, art in the White House, first ladies, first families, and much more.

POTUS—Presidents of the United States
http://www.ipl.org/ref/POTUS/
In this Web site you will find background information, election results, cabinet members, presidency highlights, and some odd facts on each of the presidents. Links to biographies, historical documents, audio and video files, and other presidential sites are also included to enrich this site.

These sites are subject to change. Go to your favorite search engine and type in United States presidents for more sites.

Pass It On

History enthusiasts: educate readers around the country by passing on information you've learned about presidents or other important people who have changed history. Share your little-known facts and interesting stories. We want to hear from you!
To get posted on the ABDO Publishing Company Web site, email us at "History@abdopub.com"
Visit the ABDO Publishing Company Web site at www.abdopub.com

Index